2 PETER AND JUDE

CONTEND FOR THE FAITH

Other studies in the Not Your Average Bible Study series

Ruth

Psalms

Jonah

Malachi

Sermon on the Mount

Ephesians

Colossians

Hebrews

James

1 Peter

1–3 John

For updates on this series, visit lexhampress.com/nyab

2 PETER & JUDE

CONTEND FOR THE FAITH

NOT YOUR AVERAGE BIBLE STUDY

JOHN D. BARRY AND MILES CUSTIS

2 Peter and Jude
Not Your Average Bible Study

Lexham Press, 1313 Commercial St., Bellingham, WA 98225
LexhamPress.com

ISBN 978-1-57-799548-7

Academic Editor (Jude): Michael S. Heiser
Managing Editor: Rebecca Van Noord
Assistant Editors: Lynnea Fraser, Abigail Stocker, Elizabeth Vince, Joel Wilcox
Cover Design: Jim LePage
Typesetting: ProjectLuz.com

CONTENTS

HOW TO USE
THIS RESOURCE

Not Your Average Bible Study is a series of in-depth Bible studies that can be used for individual or group study. Depending on your individual needs or your group pace, you may opt to cover one lesson a week or more.

Each lesson prompts you to dig deep into the Word—as such, we recommend you use your preferred translation with this study. The authors included quotations from the English Standard Version. Whatever Bible version you use, please be sure you leave ample time to get into the Bible itself.

To assist you, we recommend using the Faithlife Study Bible, which is also written and edited by John D. Barry and Miles Custis. You can download this digital resource for free for your tablet, phone, personal computer, or use it online. Go to FaithlifeBible.com to learn more.

May God bless you in the study of His Word.

INTRODUCTION

Chills run down your spine. You begin to sweat a little. Lies are being spoken—and you know it. But are you ready to do something? Do you have the courage to act on these feelings?

Subtle lies can creep into our lives under the guise of sincerity and truth. And while these influences might be difficult to discern, their effects can be devastating—lies can destroy families, churches, and communities. Presenting the truth in love and sincerity is a pillar of being a Christian.

Jude and Peter warn that we cannot be lethargic in our faith. We will be susceptible to untruth—unless we actively seek to grow.

In this study, we will learn how pursuing God through prayer, understanding Him through His Word, and relying on the Holy Spirit form our best defense against false teaching. We will see God's view of the world and our place within it. We will understand what it means to contend for the faith.

JUDE 1-13; 2 PETER 2-3

When Jude sat down to compose his letter, he wanted to write about salvation, but felt compelled to caution his audience about false teachers who had slipped into their congregation (v. 3-4). His descriptions paint a scathing portrait of these spiritual charlatans. Stealthy and crafty, they presented themselves as bearers of the good news. Defensive walls wouldn't have helped the community Jude addressed, because these leaders were already inside.

Second Peter picks up on the same message as Jude. We don't know whether Jude or 2 Peter was written first, but they do contain many of the same words—nearly verbatim at times. Since 2 Peter is significantly longer, it is likely that Peter adapted the words of Jude. As such, this study interweaves Jude and 2 Peter, reading parallel passages together. Since Jude is the shorter (and likely earlier) letter, we will first work through it in its entirety—returning at the end to the remaining passages unique to 2 Peter.

Both books contain a sense of urgency: for Jude, to proclaim salvation as it is meant to be understood; for Peter, to make preparations for Christians before he dies. For both, false leaders are the main problem to be addressed.

READING JUDE

Pray that God will give you wisdom as you study the letter of Jude.

Read the entire letter of Jude aloud in one sitting.

Jude, like most New Testament letters, was written to an entire church (or several churches). It would have been read aloud to the gathered community. Reading the letter aloud (or listening to someone read it) helps you experience it in the same way as its original recipients.

Think about Jude's purpose in writing the letter. What groups does he identify? What does he say about them?

_____

_____

_____

Note every time Jude refers to his recipients ("you"). What does he remind them of? What does he warn them about?

_____

_____

_____

_____

What specific instructions does Jude give his recipients? How can you apply his instructions to your life?

_____

_____

_____

Jude and 2 Peter have many similarities. Compare 2 Peter 2–3 to Jude. What themes do they share? How do the letters differ?

_____

_____

_____

What do Peter and Jude's parallel warnings against false teachers suggest? (Compare 2 Peter 3:14–18 with Jude 20–25.) How do the two writers encourage their readers to avoid false teachings?

_____

_____

_____

CONTENDING FOR THE FAITH

Pray that the spirit will strengthen you as you "contend for the faith."

Read Jude 1–7. Reflect on Jude 1–4.

Jude opens his letter by identifying himself and addressing his recipients. Note how he describes himself and his audience in Jude 1. Would you describe yourself as a "servant of Jesus Christ"? What does it mean to be Christ's servant?

_____

_____

_____

What does Jude's description of the recipients of his letter reveal about God? What is the relationship between being a servant of Christ and being "called," "beloved," and "kept"?

_____

_____

_____

In stating his intention to deal with the false teachers in their midst, Jude uses the Greek word *epagōnizomai* (ἐπαγωνίζομαι, "to contend"), a word often used in reference to athletic competitions. What does it mean to "contend for the faith"? Read 1 Timothy 6:12 and 1 Corinthians 9:24–27. How do these passages contribute to your understanding of what it means to contend for the faith?

_____

_____

_____

How does Jude describe the false teachers in Jude 3–4? The word *aselgeia* (ἀσέλγεια, "licentiousness" or "sensuality") typically refers to sexual immorality. What does it mean that these false teachers changed "the grace of our God into sensuality"?

_____

_____

_____

How do you enjoy freedom in Christ while avoiding sin (compare Galatians 5:13 and 1 Peter 2:16)?

_____

_____

_____

Jude says these false teachers crept in "unnoticed." How do you think false teachers were able to slip unnoticed into the community? What steps can you take to ensure you are not influenced by false teaching?

_____

_____

_____

GOD DOESN'T SLEEP

✋ *Pray that the Spirit will help you discern truth from falsehood.*

📄 *Read 2 Peter. Reflect on 2 Peter 2:1–3.*

Read the appendix, "Peter a Plagiarizer?" by Christopher R. Smith, which explains Peter's usage of Jude and identifies the parallels.

Paralleling Jude 4–5, 2 Peter notes that like false teachers are present in the church(es) he is addressing, false prophets were present in ancient Israel (2 Pet 2:1; see Lesson 4 for an explanation of the analogy in 2 Pet 2:1). How do false teachers introduce their ideas and what are the results of their efforts?

Like Jude, Peter notes that false teachers even go to the point of denying our sovereign (saving) God. What is the motivating factor for these false teachers to make such statements (2 Pet 2:2)?

Why does Peter relate "greed" and "sensuality" (2 Pet 2:2–3)? How are greed and misplaced sexual desire related issues? What does this parallel reveal about our own behavior, as well as that of false teachers? What does "greed" cause people to do? How should we address the greed in our own hearts?

_____

_____

_____

_____

_____

Read Psalm 121:1–4. How does this psalm parallel the end of 2 Peter 2:3?

_____

_____

_____

_____

We can take comfort in that God does not sit idly by while false teachers mislead His people; instead, He has already condemned their actions. God is not asleep; instead, He is taking action. God has been condemning false teachers since long ago and will continue to do so. In what ways can you take a more active role in discerning truth from falsehood?

_____

_____

_____

_____

GOD'S JUDGMENT IN HISTORY

🤲 *Pray that God will guard you from temptation.*

📄 *Read Jude 1–13. Reflect on Jude 5–7.*

Jude reminds his readers of three Old Testament events that demonstrated God's judgment on those who opposed Him. First, Jude refers to the exodus. What does Jude say about Jesus' role in that event? Compare 1 Corinthians 10:1–4. How do these verses influence your idea of Jesus' role in Old Testament events?

_____

_____

_____

_____

Read Numbers 14:1–35. Despite being delivered out of slavery in a miraculous way, the wilderness generation showed a lack of faith. What does this say about the perseverance necessary to maintain our faith?

_____

_____

_____

Read 1 Corinthians 10:5–13. How does the example of the wilderness generation encourage you to remain faithful? How can you guard against temptation?

_____

_____

_____

The second Old Testament event Jude mentions is angels leaving their "proper dwelling place." This image refers to an early Jewish understanding of the "sons of God" in Genesis 6:1–4. How do false teachers go beyond their proper authority, like the "sons of God" did? ("Angels" and "sons of God" seem to be synonymous terms in Jude and 2 Peter.) What does God's punishment of the angels in Jude 6 say about His attitude toward false teachers?

_____

_____

_____

_____

The third Old Testament example Jude uses is God's punishment of Sodom and Gomorrah. The destruction of these evil cities is recorded in Genesis 19:23–29. What does that event teach you about the seriousness of sin?

_____

_____

_____

_____

Note the progression of judgment in these three examples: "destroyed" (Jude 5), "kept in eternal chains" (v. 6), "a punishment of eternal fire" (v. 7). How do these judgments warn against false teaching? What does Jude say about God's attitude toward those who preach false things about Him? In what ways will this change your actions today and in the future?

_____

_____

_____

_____

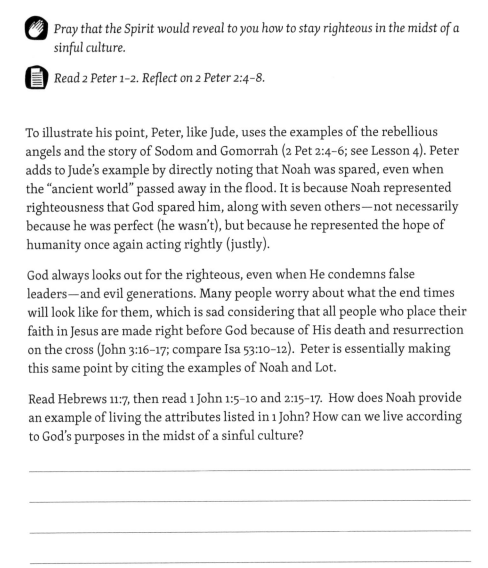

CONFRONTING SIN

Pray that the Spirit would reveal to you how to stay righteous in the midst of a sinful culture.

Read 2 Peter 1–2. Reflect on 2 Peter 2:4–8.

To illustrate his point, Peter, like Jude, uses the examples of the rebellious angels and the story of Sodom and Gomorrah (2 Pet 2:4–6; see Lesson 4). Peter adds to Jude's example by directly noting that Noah was spared, even when the "ancient world" passed away in the flood. It is because Noah represented righteousness that God spared him, along with seven others—not necessarily because he was perfect (he wasn't), but because he represented the hope of humanity once again acting rightly (justly).

God always looks out for the righteous, even when He condemns false leaders—and evil generations. Many people worry about what the end times will look like for them, which is sad considering that all people who place their faith in Jesus are made right before God because of His death and resurrection on the cross (John 3:16–17; compare Isa 53:10–12). Peter is essentially making this same point by citing the examples of Noah and Lot.

Read Hebrews 11:7, then read 1 John 1:5–10 and 2:15–17. How does Noah provide an example of living the attributes listed in 1 John? How can we live according to God's purposes in the midst of a sinful culture?

What was Lot tormented by (2 Pet 2:7–8)? Have you ever experienced similar circumstances? What did you do to stay faithful? How could you have improved the circumstances? If you fell short in the moment (like Lot, in Genesis 19:6–8), what would you cite as the main failure?

_____

_____

_____

_____

_____

GOD WILL DELIVER JUSTICE

Pray that God will lead you to understand why He is (and must be) the judge of all.

Read 2 Peter 1–2 once more. Reflect on 2 Peter 2:9–10a.

How will God respond to those who do not seek Jesus and continue to live in their sins, leading others astray (2 Pet 2:9)?

_____

_____

_____

_____

Peter's use of "defiling passion" (μιασμός, *miasmos*) is a reference to rape (particularly homosexual rape), alluding to the sinfulness of the mob in Genesis 19:5 (2 Pet 2:10). Peter likely targets this particular heinous crime because he is once again alluding to the story of Lot escaping Sodom and Gomorrah. Peter is also careful to add that these sexually immoral people also "despise authority." He likely has God's authority in mind. The people who are kept "under punishment until the day of judgment" are those who have gone against God and never repented (2 Pet 2:9). They refuse to come to Jesus and change their actions. On top of that, these people under judgment have inflicted hideous sexual crimes against others—making them especially targeted in God's judgment. The big idea: Justice will be served, so leave that to God.

When horrific crimes are committed, God knows. At times, it may feel or seem that He is not acting, but evil will be judged. God offers hope to all—even terribly sinful people—in Jesus. But for those that do not come to Him, they will be punished.

Read Luke 18:1–8. What evils committed against you do you need to hand over to God, so that He may be the judge against those who hurt you? God can offer you healing and He can be your advocate.

_____

_____

_____

IDENTIFYING FALSE LEADERS

Pray that God would teach you how to recognize false leaders.

Read 2 Peter 2. Reflect on 2 Peter 2:10b–11.

After reflecting upon evil people of the past (see 2 Pet 2:4–10a), Peter turns his focus back to the false leaders present in the church. Peter doesn't explicitly make this transition in focus, but the context seems to imply it (as do parallels with Jude, which shifts tense here to indicate a discussion of present matters). The fact that Peter doesn't make the transition explicit likely shows that as far as their characters are concerned, there is little difference between present false leaders and past evil people.

The false leaders of Peter's generation claim to have incredible authority—even spiritual beings wouldn't claim as much authority as they do (2 Pet 2:10–11). The primary context of 2 Peter is a debate about Christ's return (see 2 Pet 3:1–13). But this isn't just an academic debate—the false leaders are using the fact that Christ has not returned yet to excuse immoral behavior, such as sexually immoral acts and greed. They may have been arguing that since Christ hadn't returned yet, He wouldn't ever—and thus judgment for humanity won't come—making it fine for people to do whatever they please. Peter shows just how wrong they truly are. Have you ever encountered people who claimed to have authority that they actually don't? What was your response to them?

_____

_____

_____

_____

_____

False leaders reveal their true selves by their actions. If someone claims to know Jesus but does not act in accordance with the way He instructed us to live, then that person is a false leader—no matter what they claim to know about Him. List the major attributes of false leaders, according to 2 Peter 2. How can you use this list in your day-to-day life when discerning truth from falsehood?

_____

_____

_____

_____

HOW TO DEAL WITH A FALSE LEADER

 Pray that God would teach you how to oppose false leaders with kindness.

 Read 2 Peter 2–3. Reflect on 2 Peter 2:12–16.

When Peter says that false leaders are "like irrational animals, creatures of instinct, born to be caught and destroyed," he doesn't mean that the leaders themselves had no choice in their decisions; his accusations imply choice on their part (2 Pet 2:12). A false leader is as dangerous as a dog with rabies—you would have no choice but to put the dog down. Peter means that the false leaders behave as badly as animals and that they should thus be excommunicated from the church.

Dealing with false leaders can be tricky, but the Bible does provide some guidelines. On the other hand, if a leader just taught falsely, or fell into a sin primarily against themselves and God (i.e., a sin that is *not* a crime against another person), then they should be asked to repent immediately. (They should also be removed from leadership for the time being.) But if a false leader does not repent, you and one other witness must bring them before others to repent (see 1 Tim 5:19–20). If a person still does not repent, you will have to ask them to leave the community (see 1 Cor 5:1–5). (Compare 1 Timothy 1:3–11; 6:3–10.)

The false leaders of Peter's days are immoral, committing sins that are harmful to others, and are excusing their own behavior. There is no hope for them in the church—at least not at this stage. But Peter is not asking the community to issue the final judgment—he is merely telling them to excuse the false leaders from the community. Final judgment is for God to issue (2 Pet 2:12b–13).

What are some of the sins that identify the false leaders in Peter's churches (2 Pet 2:13–14; compare Lessons 5 and 6 for explanations of the terminology)? How do these sins act as indicators of false leaders to us today? False leaders also add to the gospel (see Titus 1:10, 16)—what does adding to the gospel mean?

_____

_____

_____

_____

Peter tells us that the fundamental identifier of these false leaders is that they have forsaken "the right way" and "gone astray" (2 Pet 2:15). To explain this, he uses the story of Balaam as an analogy. Read the story of Numbers 22–24 and 31:16. What does the story of Balaam show about God's view of false leaders and the extent he will go to in order to correct them (compare 2 Pet 2:16)?

_____

_____

_____

_____

In the process of this study, have you identified any false leaders in your life? Have you drifted into some attributes of false leadership? How do you plan to correct your actions and the actions of others?

_____

_____

_____

_____

SELFISH SHEPHERD

✋ *Pray that Christ's love will encourage you to love others humbly.*

📄 *Read Jude 3–13. Reflect on Jude 8–13.*

After reminding his readers of God's past acts of judgment, Jude continues to describe the false teachers who have infiltrated the community. What three sins does Jude attribute to false teachers in Jude 8? Are these sins related? In what ways?

_____

_____

_____

Is there any relationship between these three sins and the three examples Jude cites in Jude 5–7?

_____

_____

_____

Jude refers to a tradition about Moses' body that is not found in the Old Testament account (compare Deut 34:5–6). The word for "blasphemous" (βλασφημία, *blasphēmia*) can refer to slander. What does it mean that Michael would not slander the devil? What does this say about the presumptuous nature of the false teachers who slander what they do not understand?

_____

_____

_____

_____

Jude compares the false teachers to three Old Testament figures (Jude 11):

- For the "way of Cain," read Genesis 4:1–16.
- For the "Baalam's error," see Numbers 22–24 and 31:16 (compare Lesson 7).
- For the "Korah's rebellion," read Numbers 16:1–35.

What characterizes these three figures?

_____

_____

_____

How do you guard against jealousy, greed and wrongful rebellion?

_____

_____

_____

How does Jude describe the false teachers in Jude 12–13? What are they guilty of? What illustrations from nature does Jude use to describe them?

_____

_____

_____

_____

What does it mean to be shepherds who feed themselves? Read Ezekiel 34:2–10 and John 10:11–18. What attributes characterize a good shepherd or leader? How can you display those characteristics in your life?

_____

_____

_____

TRULY FREE IN CHRIST

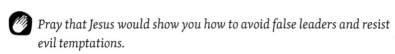 *Pray that Jesus would show you how to avoid false leaders and resist evil temptations.*

 *Read 2 Peter 2 once more. Reflect on 2 Peter 2:17–22.*

False leaders are "waterless springs and mists driven by a storm. For them the gloom of utter darkness has been reserved" (2 Pet 2:17). At times, it is difficult to understand why evil people prevail, but Peter offers us the hope that justice will be served (compare Lessons 5 and 6).

In Lessons 6 and 7, we dealt with the problems of false leaders and how to identify them. In 2 Peter 2:18–22, we are offered an even more detailed list of attributes of false leaders. What are three things that the false leaders of Peter's lifetime were doing (2 Pet 2:18–19)?

_____

_____

_____

_____

Christians are meant to be free in Christ. When Peter says it is worse to be entangled in evil after receiving Christ than to be entangled in it before receiving him, he does not seem to have general degenerative behavior in mind. Peter has in mind the evil actions of false leaders. False leaders not only commit evil after coming to Christ; they enslave others in committing evil too. False leaders use their faith as an excuse for themselves and others to commit evil. Thus, it is worse for false leaders upon the judgment day than it would have been had they never come to Christ at all—they know and have experienced the truth, but do evil against God and others anyway (2 Pet 2:21–22). Christ has died on their behalf, and they know it, but they use that as an excuse for their evil (compare Heb 5:11–6:12).

Peter points out that many people believe they are free, when they are in fact enslaved: "For whatever overcomes a person, to that he is enslaved" (2 Pet 2:19). What do you need freedom from? What is standing between you and God? Confess it to someone else and ask a group of true Christian leaders—ideally, your church elders—to pray over you, that you may be free.

_____

_____

_____

_____

JUDE 14–25; 2 PETER 3

We've all felt as though we're floundering about: things don't seem to be going right and the only changes are for the worse. People tell us to grit our teeth and pull ourselves up by our bootstraps, but we just don't have the energy to keep going—we can't muster the strength.

Without the voice of God speaking into our circumstances, our difficulties feel even more enormous. We wonder where God is—what is He doing, and why can't He just return? We ask, "Where are You, Jesus, in the midst of all this?"

But the reason Jesus hasn't returned yet will change your life for the better; it will bring you comfort and new hope.

THE LORD'S COMING

Pray that the Spirit will make you righteous in both word and deed.

Read Jude 3–16. Reflect on Jude 14–16.

As Jude continues his description of the false teachers, he refers to a prophecy by Enoch. The Old Testament records very little information about Enoch (see Gen 5:18–24). The prophecy Jude mentions is found in the book of *1 Enoch*, part of a collection of Jewish and Christian writings known as the pseudepigrapha. How does Enoch's prophecy in Jude 14–15 describe the Lord's coming?

_____

_____

_____

Jesus spoke about the coming of the "Son of Man" in Matthew 25:31–46. What is the purpose of the coming of the Lord in these passages? On what is God executing judgment?

_____

_____

_____

_____

What is the significance of God's judging of both deeds and words? What steps can you take to ensure that both your actions and your words are righteous?

_____

_____

_____

How does Jude describe false teachers in Jude 16? Which sin in the list stands out to you? Do any aspects of this description apply to you? How can you be intentional about avoiding the sins on this list?

_____

_____

_____

How can you be proactive about pursuing God and the things that please Him?

_____

_____

_____

A REMINDER

Pray that God will make your church unified in his purpose.

Read Jude 5–19. Read 2 Peter 3:1–6. Reflect on Jude 17–19.

After discussing the false teachers, Jude addresses his audience directly in Jude 17. Note how he addresses the recipients of his letter. What do you think he means when he calls them "beloved" or "dear friends"? Compare this term with his description of them in Jude 1.

_____

_____

Jude reminds his audience about the apostles' prediction that ungodly scoffers would come into the community. Earlier, Jude said that the false teachers crept in stealthily, or "unnoticed" (Jude 4). How do you think the reminder would have encouraged Jude's audience? Do prophecies fulfilled in the Bible encourage your faith? In what way?

_____

_____

_____

Peter echoes Jude's words, noting that we should "remember the predictions of the holy prophets and the commandment of the Lord and Savior through your apostles" (2 Pet 3:2). He prefaces this by stating the goal of his letter. What is Peter's goal (2 Pet 3:1)? What role does remembering God's work in the past play in our present lives?

_____

_____

_____

When Peter speaks of the apostles' prediction that scoffers would come, he gives more details about the mockers' derision. Read 2 Peter 3:2–7. Why does Peter say people will scoff? What fact do the scoffers overlook—and why does Peter emphasize this point (2 Pet 3:5; compare 2 Pet 2:4–10a)?

_____

_____

_____

How and why do people mock Christianity today?

_____

_____

_____

How does Jude describe the scoffers in Jude 19? Paul often warns against those who create division within the church (see Rom 16:17; 1 Cor 1:10; 3:1–9; 12:24–26; Titus 3:10–11). Why do you think the New Testament letters stress the importance of unity within the church?

_____

_____

_____

Would you characterize your church as united or divided? How can you pray for unity? What actions can you take to foster unity in your community?

_____

_____

_____

_____

INSTRUCTIONS

Pray for spiritual maturity as you seek to be built up in faith.

Read Jude 17–23. Reflect on Jude 20–23.

As he closes his letter, Jude gives his readers some instructions in verses 20–21. How would these instructions have helped Jude's audience guard against false teachers?

_____

_____

_____

_____

What are ways you can build yourself up in faith? How can others help build you up?

_____

_____

_____

_____

How can you help build others up in their faith? What role does prayer have in this?

_____

_____

_____

_____

What is the relationship between the two instructions Jude gives in Jude 21 (compare 1 John 4:9)?

_____

_____

_____

Read John 15:10 and 1 John 2:15; 3:17. What do these verses say about being in God's love? How can you ensure that you are keeping yourself in God's love?

_____

_____

_____

_____

In Jude 20–21, Jude refers to all three members of the Trinity ("the Holy Spirit," "God," and "Lord Jesus Christ"). What features does Jude attribute to each one? How often do you think about each member of the Godhead?

_____

_____

_____

_____

How are you "praying in the Holy Spirit" (v. 20)? How do you keep yourself "in the love of God" (v. 21)? How are you "waiting for the mercy of our Lord Jesus Christ" (v. 21)?

_____

_____

_____

_____

Jude lists three ways of reacting to others in Jude 22–23. What are the ways? What does it mean to "have mercy on those who doubt"? How does that differ from showing "mercy with fear" to others?

_____

_____

_____

_____

Can you think of someone in your life who is in one of the above groups? How should you reach out to this person?

_____

_____

_____

_____

JESUS' DELAYED RETURN

Pray that Jesus would reveal to you why "the end" is relevant to your life now.

Read 2 Peter 2–3. Reflect on 2 Peter 3:7–15a.

Just as Noah's flood came through a prophetic word, so the end of the world will also come—for God has spoken it (2 Pet 3:7; compare Lesson 5). On the day that Jesus returns, evil will be completely removed from the earth. It is very difficult to understand why Jesus said that day would come soon when it has not come yet (nearly 2,000 years later). But Peter tells us this is because "with the Lord one day is as a thousand years, and a thousand years as one day" (2 Pet 3:8). According to Peter, what is the reason why Jesus has not returned (2 Pet 3:9)? (The "you" in 2 Peter 3:9 is a plural in Greek—meaning "you all." This means that he intends to address his entire audience, and by extension, the entire world.)

_____

_____

_____

_____

How will the "day of the Lord" actually come (2 Pet 3:10)? In light of the context of 2 Peter chapter 2, what type of "works" do you think Peter means will be exposed on that day?

_____

_____

_____

_____

_____

With the "day of the Lord" in our focus, how then should we live today
(2 Pet 3:10–12, 14)?

_____

_____

_____

When the new heaven and new earth are created, righteousness will dwell
on the earth—meaning that all injustice will be judged and right living will
rule the earth (2 Pet 3:13). This is what justice ultimately means and looks like.
What can we practically do today—as individuals and as communities—to be
living on the last day in a way that would make Jesus proud (2 Pet 3:14)?

_____

_____

_____

_____

How should we view the time between now and the last day (2 Pet 3:15a)?
How should we practically respond to God in the time that we have been given?

_____

_____

_____

_____

WHERE PETER AND PAUL MEET

🤲 *Pray that the Spirit would reveal to you how the difficult parts of Scripture provide great reward.*

📄 *Read 2 Peter 3. Reflect on 2 Peter 3:15b–16.*

In 2 Peter 3:15, Peter tells us that his message about the day of the Lord directly parallels that of the Apostle Paul's. This is because Paul also viewed the delay of Christ's coming as demonstrative of His patience with humanity. Like Peter, Paul viewed Jesus' delayed return as an opportunity to live fully for God now. Read Romans 2:4 and 9:22–24. Which message is clearer to you—Peter's or Paul's (compare Lesson 11)?

_____

_____

_____

_____

Peter also notes that Paul's words can at times be difficult to understand—and thus are susceptible to people twisting them for their own gain. Peter's note on this matter is likely meant to illustrate once again the problem with false leaders—they will even use Scripture, and Jesus Himself, as an excuse for evil (2 Pet 3:16; compare Lessons 5 and 6).

_____

_____

_____

_____

What are some practical solutions to dealing with passages of Scripture that are difficult to understand?

_____

_____

_____

Who should you check your opinions about Scripture against? Who should you check the opinions of others against? How can you easily identify teachings that are not in accordance with God's will (again compare Lessons 5 and 6)?

_____

_____

_____

_____

DOXOLOGY

Pray that god will give you a greater understanding of his glory, majesty, power and authority.

Read Jude 1–25. Read 2 Peter 3:17–18. Reflect on Jude 24–25.

Instead of a benediction or final greetings (compare 1 Cor 16:23–24, Heb 13:20–21), Jude closes his letter with a doxology. A doxology is a liturgical formula of praise ascribing glory and honor to God. How does Jude describe God in his doxology? Why is glory due to Him?

_____

_____

_____

What aspects of Jude's doxology show God's concern for us?

_____

_____

_____

How does God help protect you from stumbling? Can you think of an example where God has done this in your life?

_____

_____

_____

_____

The Greek word for "blameless" (ἄμωμος, amōmos) is often used in the Greek version of the Old Testament to refer to an unblemished sacrifice (see Num 6:14). The word is used in the New Testament to describe Christ's perfect sacrifice (see Heb 9:14, 1 Pet 1:19). How does Christ's sacrifice allow us to stand blameless before God's glory?

_____

_____

_____

_____

According to Peter's closing remarks, what things should we look out for (2 Pet 3:17)? What things should we do instead (2 Pet 3:18)?

_____

_____

_____

_____

There are several other doxologies in the New Testament:

- Romans 11:33–36; 16:25–27

- Ephesians 3:20–21

- 1 Timothy 1:17

- Revelation 5:13

What are some similarities among these doxologies? What are some differences?

_____

_____

_____

_____

Try composing your own doxology. What attributes of God would you include? Why are these attributes important to you?

_____

_____

_____

_____

2 PETER 1

Self-reflection is healthy, but can also be scary—it usually results in serious changes in our lives. When Peter opened his second letter, he didn't just have change in mind: He wanted to see his audience transform their lives to be more like Christ.

For all our talk about transformation, we still don't really comprehend what it means to be transformed. What would it mean for us to embrace change in our entire lives as we commune with Him through prayer, worship, community, and digging into the Bible—to live the way He lived, with our lives fully dictated by the wonderful agenda of God?

With God, we can become more than we could ever imagine. And that's a beautiful thing. Because with God, entire communities can be changed for the better.

Peter is essentially asking us: Who do you want to be, really? Let's journey back to the beginning of his letter and discover what it really means to be a Christian.

YOU'RE A CHRISTIAN— HERE'S WHAT THAT MEANS

Pray that God would give you an inspiring outlook on your life—one completely motivated by living for Him.

Read all of 2 Peter. Reflect on 2 Peter 1:1-4.

How does Peter identify himself (compare Lesson 2)? What does his self-identification indicate about how we should view ourselves before God?

_____

_____

_____

According to Peter, what type of faith have Christians received and *how* did we receive it (2 Pet 1:1)?

_____

_____

_____

Faith in Christ is meant to offer godliness to us and others. What has Christ's divine power granted to us (2 Pet 1:3-4)? What are the practical implications of this in our lives?

_____

_____

_____

_____

How does our acceptance of Christ's work set us apart?

_____

_____

_____

_____

WHEN YOU COME TO THE END

Pray that the idea of Jesus returning would give you perspective on your current circumstances and practices.

Read all of 2 Peter 1. Reflect on 2 Peter 1:4–15.

Peter lists a sequence of connections between faith and other virtues (2 Pet 1:5–7). Take time to write down this sequence on a small card and carry it in your pocket this week as a reminder of what Jesus intends for you to be. Note on the card that you are a partaker "of the divine nature." Through Christ, you have the very power of God to live these virtues.

_____

_____

_____

What ability do the virtues (qualities) that Peter lists in 1:5–7 provide us (2 Pet 1:8)? What is the result of lacking these virtues (2 Pet 1:9)?

_____

_____

_____

When Peter says that you should be diligent "to confirm your calling and election," he does not mean that our salvation is dependent upon these actions—our salvation is dependent on Jesus alone (John 3:16; compare Isa 53:12). Likewise, when Peter says that "in this way there will be *richly provided* for you an entrance into the eternal kingdom of our Lord," he does not mean that living by these actions provides an entrance into God's Kingdom (2 Pet 3:11). Instead, Peter means that we should work towards living as if we are actually saved—so that our entrance into God's kingdom will be rich and beautiful. Living the virtues listed in 2 Peter 1:5–7 sets us up for success rather than failure (2 Pet 1:10). The big question behind what Peter is saying is:

When you go to heaven, or when Jesus returns again, what do you want him to say? Do you want to hear Jesus say, "Well done, good and faithful servant," or to suddenly realize that although you are "saved," you could have done much more for God while on earth—having brought others to Him in the process?

_____

_____

_____

In 2 Peter 1:12–13, we get a glimpse of Peter as a pastor: Why does Peter make his statements in 2 Peter 1:3–11? Peter is writing this book at the end of his life, with the knowledge that he will soon be departing the world (2 Pet 1:14–15). If you were at the end of your life, what would you remind people of?

_____

_____

_____

WE HAVE SEEN IT WITH OUR OWN EYES

Pray that the Spirit would inspire you to live your life as if you had seen Jesus face to face.

Read 2 Peter 1 once more. Reflect on 2 Peter 1:16–18.

Against the myths perpetuated by false leaders—which Peter notes are "clever" (i.e., surprisingly deceptive)—Peter tells us how he came to his revelations (2 Pet 1:16–18). What sets Peter apart from false leaders—and how can we as modern Christians depend on similar ideas (2 Pet 1:16; compare Luke 1:1–4)? (Peter is alluding to Jesus' baptism and transfiguration: Read Mark 1:9–11 and 9:2–8.)

_____

_____

_____

_____

_____

Peter is likely contrasting his viewpoint with the ideas of Graeco-Roman mythology (compare 1 Tim 1:4). Considering the types of sins the false leaders were committing, listed throughout the book, it's possible that these false leaders may have treated Jesus as a type of Graeco-Roman god. If this were the case, they may have been developing a Graeco-Roman style cult religion around Him—or at the very least, excusing (in Jesus' name) indulging in the behaviors of their culture. When Peter says that we are "partakers of the divine nature," he is directly contrasting his viewpoint with that of Graeco-Roman religions (2 Pet 1:4). Graeco-Roman religious practices often suggested that humans could become gods. In Christianity, believers *share in* divinity by being part of God's family—through Jesus' saving acts—but do not become gods themselves (compare Rom 8:29). In what ways do other religious viewpoints creep into the church today? How can you identify them over and against the actual teachings of Jesus?

_____

_____

_____

_____

What are some ways you can kindly—and in Christ's love—address the problem of heresies?

_____

_____

_____

_____

THE POWER OF THE PROPHETIC WORD

🤲 *Pray that the Spirit would inspire you to live your life immersed in God's Word.*

📄 *Read all of 2 Peter once more. Reflect on 2 Peter 1:19-21.*

In our generation, many Christians act as if heresies aren't a big deal. We're deeply troubled when corruption in the church becomes public—or when a Christian leader commits a terrible sin—but we're not very cautious about the actual teachings in our communities. But for Peter, all of the major sins within the Christian community were directly rooted in the evil taught by false leaders. For this reason, Peter tells us that we have something more sure than even witnessing Jesus ourselves: "the prophetic word" (2 Pet 1:19). By the prophetic word, Peter means God speaking through the Scriptures; we can use the Word for discernment. "Morning star" is a metaphor for Jesus. Why should we pay attention to the prophetic word? What sets it apart? What is the effect of God's Word in our lives (2 Pet 1:19-20)?

_____

_____

_____

Read Isaiah 6:1-13. Compare 2 Peter 1:20-21. What sets apart a prophet's work and words? How is the prophetic word—the Old Testament words of the prophets and by extension the entire Bible—a sure measure for words spoken today?

_____

_____

_____

_____

What parts of your spiritual life and practice is God calling you to change today? What teachings are you abiding by that are not in alignment with the Bible's teachings? How can you be more careful with the information you take in as truth?

_____

_____

_____

_____

CONCLUSION

We live in a world swarming with opinions and ideas that oppose God's desire. It's all too easy to let these influences inch into our hearts and beliefs.

Jesus should shine in us like a lamp in a dark place. We should be filled with His Word, so that it can speak into us and into the lives of others (2 Pet 1:19–20). We are called, beloved, and kept by God so that we might pursue Him.

Jude suggests an antidote for spiritual lethargy and false teachings: We can build ourselves up in the faith by praying in the Holy Spirit, keeping ourselves and others in the love of God, and looking forward to the eternal life we enjoy through Christ's sacrifice (Jude 20–21). But ultimately, as Jude points out, the best protection from temptation comes from relying on God, "who is able to keep you from stumbling and to present you blameless before the presence of his glory with great joy" (v. 24).

Peter elaborates on Jude's message, telling us that God is the great rescuer in all situations. In Jesus, we can overcome sin and destruction; we can even overcome heretics and their heresies through the godliness that comes when Christ transforms our lives.

Jesus' love provides the protection from evil that we all need—in this very moment, Jesus speaks truth into our lives through His prophetic word. In Christ, we find faith and become virtuous (2 Pet 1:19; compare 1:5–7). Our knowledge of Jesus leads us to self-control and makes us steadfast. And in our steadfastness, through God's great strength, we become godly. Godliness is the answer our world needs—the answer that shows true compassion and love (2 Pet 1:5–8).

May God bless you and keep you—and may He make his face to shine upon you—as you live by the teaching of His word and abide in His Holy Spirit.

PETER A PLAGIARIZER?

Christopher R. Smith

If the Bible is God's unchanging Word, why would Peter use some of Jude's words, and then change them?

Right in the middle of Peter's second letter, he takes the letter of Jude and adapts it, section by section—in sequence. He not only uses Jude's ideas, but the same words and phrases, but with an interesting twist—he changes their order, context and application. Is this an ancient example of plagiarism?

(Words in **bold** type are those that Peter and Jude have in common.)[1]

Jude	2 Peter
For certain individuals whose **condemnation** (κρίμα, *krima*) was written about **long** ago have **secretly** slipped in among you. They are ungodly people, who pervert the grace of our God into a license for **immorality** (ἀσέλγεια, *aslegia*) and **deny** Jesus Christ our only **Sovereign** (δεσπότης, *despotes*) and Lord. ... The Lord at one time delivered his **people** out of Egypt, but later **destroyed** those who did not believe (4–5).	But there were also false prophets among the **people**, just as there will be false teachers among you. They will **secretly** introduce destructive heresies, even **denying** the **sovereign** Lord (δεσπότης, *despotes*) who bought them—bringing swift destruction on themselves. Many will follow their **depraved conduct** (ἀσέλγεια, *aslegia*) and will bring the way of truth into disrepute. ... Their **condemnation** (κρίμα, *krima*) has **long** been hanging over them, and their **destruction** has not been sleeping (2:1-3).
PETER'S USE OF JUDE	
Peter uses the same analogy as Jude to account for the presence of false teachers among true believers: Some unfaithful people came out of Egypt with Israel, but they perished in the wilderness. Peter says the same four things Jude says about these false teachers: They act secretly; they deny the "sovereign one" (δεσπότης, *despotes*);[2] they are immoral; and their "condemnation" or "judgment" (κρίμα, *krima*) was determined long ago.	

[1] All verses cited from the New International Version (NIV).

[2] The term *despotes* is rarely applied to God in the New Testament, and is used nowhere else in Peter's letters.

Jude	2 Peter
And the **angels** who did not keep their positions of authority but abandoned their proper dwelling— these he has kept in **darkness**, bound with everlasting **chains** for **judgment** on the great Day. In a similar way, **Sodom and Gomorrah** … serve as an **example** of those who suffer the punishment of eternal fire (6–7).	For if God did not spare **angels** when they sinned, but sent them to hell, putting them into **chains of darkness** to be held for **judgment** … if he condemned the cities of **Sodom and Gomorrah** by burning them to ashes, and made them an **example** of what is going to happen to the ungodly (2:4, 6).

PETER'S USE OF JUDE

Peter follows Jude in using the rebellious angels and the cities of Sodom and Gomorrah as examples of God's judgment. But Peter adds the example of the judgment during Noah's flood. He also cites Noah and Lot as people who were spared. His point: God will protect the righteous when He judges the wicked (2:4–9).

Jude	2 Peter
These ungodly people … reject **authority** and **heap abuse on celestial beings**. But **even the archangel** Michael … said, "The **Lord** rebuke you!" Yet these people **slander** (βλασφημέω, blaspheme) **whatever they do not understand;** and the very things they do understand by **instinct**—as **irrational animals do**—will **destroy** (φθείρω, phtheir) them (8–10).	Those who follow the corrupt desire of the flesh … despise **authority**. Bold and arrogant, they are not afraid to **heap abuse on celestial beings; yet even angels** … do not heap abuse on such beings when bringing judgment on them from the **Lord**. But these people **blaspheme** (βλασφημέω, blaspheme) in **matters they do not understand**. They are like **unreasoning animals**, creatures of **instinct** … and like animals they too will **perish** (φθεύρω, phtheir) (2:10–12).

PETER'S USE OF JUDE

Both Jude and Peter were appalled by the arrogance and rebellion of the false teachers since even angels don't claim to have such authority.

Jude	2 Peter
Woe to them! They have taken the **way** of Cain; they have rushed for **profit** (μισθός, *misthos*) into **Balaam's error** (πλάνη, *plane*); they have been destroyed in Korah's rebellion. These people are **blemishes** (σπιλάς, *spilas*) at your love **feasts**, eating with you without the slightest qualm (11–12).	They are **blots** (σπιλάς, *spilas*) and blemishes, reveling in their pleasures while they **feast** with you.... They have left the straight way and **wandered off** (πλανάω, *planaō*)[3] to follow the **way** of **Balaam** son of Bezer, who loved the **wages** (μισθός, *misthos*) of wickedness (2:13, 15).

PETER'S USE OF JUDE

Like Jude, Peter describes the false teachers as "blemishes" (σπιλάς, *spilas*) at the community's feasts and compares them to Balaam (Num 22–24). But Peter doesn't pick up Jude's examples of Cain and Korah. Instead, he develops the Balaam example (2:15–16).

Jude	2 Peter
They are clouds **without rain** (ἄνυδρος, *anudros*), **blown along by the wind;** autumn trees, without fruit and uprooted—twice dead. They are wild waves of the sea, foaming up their shame; wandering stars, for whom **blackest darkness** has been **reserved** forever (12–13).	These people are springs **without water** (ἄνυδρος, *anudros*) and mists **driven by a storm.** **Blackest darkness** is **reserved** for them (2:17).

PETER'S USE OF JUDE

Peter follows Jude closely here—borrowing his vivid imagery. But Peter uses fewer images to make his own point.[4]

---

[3] The verb *plane* and the noun *planaō* are derived from the same letters, and have the same range of meaning.

[4] Peter doesn't repeat Jude's quotation from the book of Enoch or its elaboration in Jude 14–16.

Jude	2 Peter
But, dear friends, remember what the **apostles** of our Lord Jesus Christ foretold. They said to you, **"In the last times there will be scoffers** who will **follow their own ungodly desires"** (17–18).	I want you to recall the words spoken in the past by the holy prophets and the command given by our Lord and Savior through your **apostles**. Above all, you must understand that **in the last days scoffers will come**, scoffing and **following their own evil desires** (3:2–3).

PETER'S USE OF JUDE

Jude's point about the "scoffers" is that they are immoral and may lead believers astray into sin. He urges believers to remain faithful and try to rescue those who are in spiritual danger. Peter makes a different point: The scoffers will deny that Jesus is coming back. Nonetheless, Peter, like Jude, urges Christ-followers to be on guard so they're not deceived.

Jude	2 Peter
To him who is able to keep you from stumbling and to present you before his glorious presence without fault and with great joy—to the only God **our Savior be glory**, majesty, power and authority, through **Jesus Christ our Lord**, before all ages, **now and forevermore! Amen** (24–25).	But grow in the grace and knowledge of **our Lord and Savior Jesus Christ**. To him **be glory** both **now and forever! Amen** (3:18).

PETER'S USE OF JUDE

Like Jude, Peter ends his second letter with a praise hymn.[5]

---

[5]By contrast, Peter's first letter ends with the standard first-century closing elements.

Does Peter's use of Jude's letter indicate that it wasn't God's Word for him?

Peter couldn't pay a higher compliment to Jude. This second letter is Peter's spiritual last will and testament. He tells his readers that he will "soon put … [his body] aside, as our Lord Jesus Christ … made clear to [him]" (1:14). So he says, "make every effort to see that after my departure you will always be able to remember these things"—the things he taught about Jesus as an "eyewitness" of his life and ministry (1:15-16). Peter is putting his apostolic authority behind everything in this letter and everything he has taught. By incorporating Jude's words, and interweaving his "apostolic" words throughout, he is testifying to the truth and authority of them— not plagiarizing.

Peter didn't change anything essential to Jude's message. Instead, he asserts that it's applicable to even wider circles than Jude originally addressed. That's treating Jude as the unchanging Word of God.

The biblical authors sometimes do things we wouldn't expect them to. But when we reflect on what they're actually doing, and why, we can understand how the Bible *really* works. We are also given a glimpse of how God's Word can be applied in different contexts, and to different groups of people.

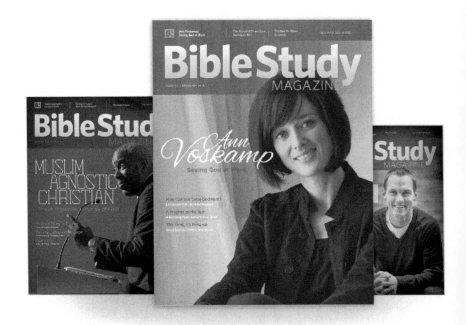